Saints & Sinners, Geniuses & Idiots:

Now What!?

Bob Bruno

This is a work of fiction. Names, characters, places, and incidents either are the product of the author's imagination or are used fictitiously. Any resemblance to actual persons, living or dead, events, or locales is entirely coincidental.

Copyright © 2024 by Bob Bruno

All rights reserved.

No part of this book may be reproduced or used in any manner without written permission of the copyright owner except for the use of quotations in a book review. For more information, address: bob@bobbruno.net.

First paperback edition April 2024

Book design by Ellen M. Potts
Map by Oscar Hannity

www.bobbruno.net

Table of Contents

Table Of Contents

Now	4
Commercial Break	20
In the Beginning, Was the Womb	34
After Birth Is Life	43
Was That a Nudge or a Shove?	64
Saints and Sinners, Geniuses and Idiots	95
Compatibility	117
Now What!?	140
About the Author	151

Now

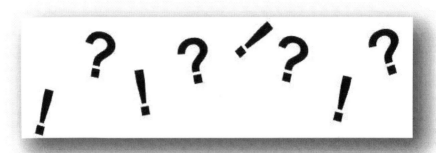

So many times we hear folks say that Dave did this bad thing or Sam did this good thing when, in fact, what Dave did was exactly the right thing for Dave to do for Dave. And Sam actually made a mistake by doing what was not going to work out well for Sam.

So often, we make comments about someone doing something right or something wrong. In fact, what many folks do is not right or wrong but something different. Why do we set these standards for this behavior being right while the other behavior is wrong? Was it something Mom or Dad said way back when? Or was it an aunt's or a grandparent's statement?

Stepping away from family, did a teacher mention something in the first or second grade that made an impression that stayed with you?

There is so much to deal with in life: growing up, getting through school, starting life as a young adult, going through temporary jobs, trying to settle down, start-up, begin a career, meet the right one, set up a family, raise them, make money. How much? Retire? Did I do it right? What now? Now what?!

Is this really necessary?

Good grief!

What am I supposed to do? What was I supposed to do? Why am I dealing with so many different kinds of stuff? What happened to what my mom, dad, aunt, grammy, or grandpa said? What happened to what I knew was normal?

Wow!

Good grief!

Is this all just so much B - - - S - - -?

NO, it's not!

The first concern is, "What is normal?" "Normal" is a relative term. If someone from northern Alaska goes to Myrtle Beach, North Carolina, he or she will think it is extremely warm. If someone from Rio de Janeiro, Brazil, goes to the same location, they may think it is a little on the cool side.

The point is some things we consider normal are relative to other folks' perceptions.

Again, "normal" is a relative term. Remember that it's all perspective. What you grew up with was your normal. What your best friend grew up with was their normal. You might be surprised to learn that there might have been drastic differences just in those two normals.

It's probably easy for you to realize that how you grew up and how your grandparents grew up was different. After all, they're so much older that life just had to be very different way back then. You might be surprised to learn that there were a lot more similarities between how they grew up then and how you grew up now than you realize. Wherever you are in the world, your normal is very different from most of the other places. It might be very different from someone who lived right down the street or even someone who lived right next door.

Another thing to consider is how some folks are born with certain conditions. Regardless of the condition, we have to understand that, for that person, it's normal. For someone born blind, that is their normal. Birthmark, normal. Skin condition, normal. Club foot, normal. Missing limb(s), normal. So, for those born with an unusual condition, they do the same, just differently. It's their normal.

For most of us, learning to walk presented a challenge. We learned, through trial and error, how to overcome the challenge. Learning to tie our shoes, brush our teeth, and respond when our name is called are all challenges that we learn to deal with and overcome.

As we mentioned earlier about how being raised next door could be a different normal, we must understand that we do not know what goes on behind closed doors. The behaviors seen in public are not necessarily the same behaviors that occur when those doors are shut. Those behaviors are normal when being raised there. Those are behaviors that you may never be aware of.

It's entirely possible that the husband and wife, the mommy and daddy to one of your friends, have a difficult, maybe even abusive, relationship. You never see it, and your friend may never say anything about it because of fear or embarrassment. That is their collective normal.

Or their family relationship is very content. Your friend's mommy and daddy get along very well, and your friend, who you always considered friendly and relaxed, assumes that everyone has a warm and loving home to go to after school. You carry some resentment because your house is not a place where you ever feel comfortable.

The fundamental concept behind all this is that there is no point that is normal. There is no numerical value, no specific behavior that is normal. The most important thing you must realize is that your normal growing up was not normal. It was not normal… NOT normal! NOT!!! NORMAL!!! Well, if it was not normal, then what was it? It was normal to you. It was normal only for you. It was not normal to anyone else.

To make sure there's no misunderstanding, you may have anywhere from a few to many behaviors that you share with other folks. BUT, there is no other individual who is exactly like you. Your actual normal is yours and only yours.

Another point requiring understanding is the complexity surrounding the differences of personalities. Suppose there are two people who we'll refer to as Tom and Sam. Tom and Sam are very popular guys. Everyone enjoys their company and loves having either of them as guests at a social function or as coworkers on a project. Both of them are polite, respectful, and just nice people to have around.

The problem is that Tom and Sam have difficulty working with each other. Within a few minutes of being together, either socially or professionally, on the job, they begin to irritate each other. This irritation builds until one or both feel a real need to get away from the other.

How can two "nice" people have issues with each other? There are no noticeable differences culturally. They might have the same religion, be close in age, share political perspectives, financial status, or social standing. So, why is there a problem between the two?

This is one of the critical issues surrounding personalities.

Without any identifiable facts that enable us to define this incompatibility, how are we to determine what is the problem?

Personalities are much more complex than what we can imagine. A seemingly trivial behavior of one person can be, for whatever reason, extremely irritating to another. The one exercising the behavior may not really notice it, while the one being irritated cannot really define why that behavior is so aggravating.

Recognizing this relatively minor difference is very critical to identifying the true complexity of an individual.

Most of us have experienced this feeling about someone else. One of the challenges in this book is for you to question yourself when you have felt irritation about someone else's behavior. What was the behavior? Why did it irritate you? Have you seen this same behavior in someone else? Did it bother you when the other person did it, or was it just when this person did it?

Many times, we've simply thought that person was a dummy. We've wondered why they couldn't see how their behavior was foolish or irritating. It was so obvious to us that we were mystified why they couldn't see it.

Take a moment and dwell on these questions. Read the previous two paragraphs again. Put some time into answering the questions. This will only be the first of several times you'll be asked to do this.

Questions like this will be asked throughout the book. Recognizing your reaction to someone's behavior is critical to achieving an understanding of other people and, just as importantly, understanding of yourself.

The goal of this book is to enable you to make more effective decisions in dealing with other people. In doing so, it provides you with an understanding of the idea that any person, at any moment may have complete justification for each and every attitude, thought, and behavior they exhibit.

Those justifications are built on their normal, their base personality. We are going to discover what that personality might be, how it started, and how it got to be the way it is.

Another important issue to deal with is realizing that you have several friends who agree with you on many issues. With the support of those friends, you will tend to create your own echo chamber. You and your friends will reinforce each other's perceptions, strengthening those feelings about those particular positions.

And, if you really pay attention, you'll notice that you tend to ignore those who disagree with you. You may talk with them about why you disagree. You may even have a heated discussion about the disagreement. After a while, you will avoid bringing up those issues with those folks since you know the discussions will only result in ongoing stalemates.

Those two behaviors, mutual agreements and disagreements, may become traps that restrict your understanding of other folks and of yourself. When you decide that you and they are fixed in these attitudes, you have ceased learning about the why.

One of the requirements for you to make this book work effectively is to realize that when you do something, your action has complete justification in your mind. It is the right thing to do. It is the most logical thing to do. It just feels right to do this or to do it in this way.

The challenge for you is to explain to yourself why this is the right way or the best available way. The "why" is the most unasked and unanswered question in our life. Until we start asking that question, we won't know any more about our actions than we did before.

Before we do that, we're going to examine how personalities get started and how they get to be the way they are.

When it is all over and done with, if you've put some thought and effort into it, then you'll have a better understanding of why you are doing what you're doing. Then, you'll have a better understanding of why he or she is doing what they're doing.

You will discover why you and they will do different things, buy different products, vote differently, belong to different religions, and treat people differently, all the while still loving and respecting (or not) each other. Yes, we will cover the "or not."

In covering these issues, you will recognize our mutual concern about feeling some level of stress in dealing with these differences. Any time we hear an opinion that differs from ours, we have a natural stress reaction. We feel a need to defend our position. In the old days, it was an issue of survival.

In the middle of all that, you may also decide that if it does not change what you're going to have for breakfast, then it's not that important to feel a level of stress about it.

It's all about understanding. You'll realize that the common phrase "walk a mile in my shoes" doesn't even scratch the surface of understanding. Without experiencing the other person's complete life experience, we will not really understand his or her emotional status and resulting behaviors.

You will realize that respect is the critical defining factor. You must extend and receive respect before there is an improvement in your mutual relationships. And this respect must continue even when it's not returned. That can become very difficult.

We are going to cover a lot of territory in the few chapters we have. Some very smart folks have written a lot about personalities. We will identify some critical points that they have described. We will not go into the level of detail that they did when they wrote about their perceptions.

Another issue to be concerned with is some all-too common phrases. We must understand that common sense is not always that common. We need to realize that NOT "everybody knows" about everything. Knowing that "I wouldn't do that!" also means "Others would." And "Why would he/she" just means "I don't know why." These and similar phrases lull us into a lazy way of thinking. We too easily assume certain things without thinking. That lack of thinking contributes to prejudice and a lack of concern or understanding about other people's feelings.

These chapters are not intended to comprise a scholarly or academic level of discussion. They are intended to give you an adequate understanding of how someone's personality starts, develops over the years, and justifies itself and the resultant behaviors. Some people pay tidy little sums to do what this book will ask you to do on your own. The requests consist of you asking yourself, "Why?"

Why "Why?"

Because answering that simple question properly is supposed by many to be the key to life. The answer to that question will not be found in this book.

It will be found in your mind, in your thoughts, about why you've done some of the things you've done. It will be found in your thinking about why you did not do something else in those situations.

Now, some of you will ask, "Why did I buy this book if I'm the one who's supposed to do the real work?" Good question.

The answer is, some of those other books claim to have the answer but, in fact, you are the only one who really knows. Some of those other books are excellent and have some superior educational benefits. But, the real answers do not really exist in this or any other book. They exist in you.

This book will provide you with some perspective along with some tools that will equip you with the ability to evaluate who you are and why. In so doing, it may enable you to understand who they are and why. The challenge in this book is to ask you the questions in such a manner that you meet that challenge honestly and fairly.

If you provide the necessary thinking, I guarantee you that you will experience some uncomfortable feelings. Honesty and truth do that to us.

The other books may provide you with some glimpses into specific aspects of certain behaviors and do it very well. But they do not bring finality.

This book goes to the core. Until you know the reason you did "this" or said "that," you will not really "have it."

You see, your thoughts and resultant behaviors are completely logical to you. They make complete sense based on your previous experiences.

This book requires you to think about your thinking. You must learn to think about how you think. You must think about why you think the way you do.

Not an easy task.

Commercial Break

What this book is NOT. This is not a replacement for treatable mental disorders. This book will not do an analysis of conditions that are covered in the Diagnostic and Statistical Manual of Mental Disorders, commonly referred to as the DSM.

While mental disorders are recognized and known to exist, they may be mentioned when discussing extreme behaviors. There will be no attempt to provide analyses on specifics of causes or treatments.

Additionally, we will be discussing most of the folks that you'll meet. In human biology, that will be the XX and XY chromosomes, not XXY, XYY, or any other deviations. Yes, they have their normal. And there are publications that deal with them. But, as mentioned, we are concerned about the majority of the people you will meet and deal with during life.

In talking about personalities, we will mention some of the terms used when people talk about other people. After all, when we describe other folks, we use some terms in private or small group discussions that are not complimentary, sometimes even insulting, terms. When these terms are used, they are in no way reflective of the people or their associated groups. They are used to illuminate how they reflect a speaker's attitude and how that usage can modify a listener's attitude or perspective.

This book is a guide to understanding why people behave the way they do. It offers frameworks to enable you to come to some sort of understanding of how different forces modify and challenge a person's behavior. One of its goals is to enable you to comprehend why your friends do something that appears to be out of character for them and possibly lower your opinion of them. But it may also explain why you see someone you did not have much respect for do something that makes you think you may have misunderstood them, that they may not be "all bad."

To develop that understanding, you will be questioned about your thoughts. You will be asked to explain those thoughts more than a few times.

Our thoughts lead to our behaviors, and, as with most routines, we develop thought patterns, thought habits. And, like most habits, that repetition results in reacting without thinking and behaving that way only because that's the way we've been doing it with no problem. As a result, we start behaving reflexively. If we have developed a certain perspective about a group, we no longer question our opinion when it comes to meeting or reading about an individual from that group.

Falling into this type of habitual thinking and the resulting habitual behavior, we no longer see the person as an individual but as a "typical" person of that "group." Sam is just another "black" or "slant-eye" or "honky". Harry is just another "Biblethumper" or "papist" or "towel-head". Joe is just another "dumb Democrat" or "cold-hearted Republican." We quit questioning our attitude and succumb to the all-too-common trap of prejudicial thinking.

If we intend to develop effective thinking, we must accept some basic concepts concerning these groups and the individuals from these groups.

The first thing we must accept is that most of these groups have subgroups, smaller groups that disagree among themselves about some issues that the big group supposedly believes, what behaviors they are supposed to follow, what perspectives they should have about other groups, including the big group they are part of.

The next thing we must accept is that the individuals within these subgroups may disagree with some of the subgroups' beliefs, the behaviors the subgroup expects, and the perspectives of the subgroups about the others.

The third and final thing we must accept is that when we get to the individual, we have to accept that each individual is unique. Some individuals may agree with other individuals about some of things but disagree with them about other things. In other words, between the religious, political, and cultural aspects, the individual has a perspective on life that is absolutely and totally unique.

Therefore, when we see another person, regardless of what group they appear to belong to, or from conversations, what group philosophy they appear to follow, we must realize that we have only discerned a tiny fraction of what that person is and what thoughts and behaviors they may tend to follow.

The acceptance of those ideas is critical to our meager grasp of what constitutes that person, their thoughts, their beliefs, and their emotional state regarding things in life.

Having said all that, it must also be accepted as obvious that many folks will do things that have absolutely no sense to support a behavior. One of the awesome things about being a human is that most of us have done something that, immediately after, we have paused and thought, "Good grief, why did I say that?" or "…do that?"

Due to the complete lack of logic, most of us have done one of these completely unexplainable actions. This is one of those rare events that may never have an explanation. It is doubtful that any book, including this one, will, by definition, make sense of a senseless action.

As mentioned earlier, the old phrase "walk a mile in my shoes…" doesn't even scratch the surface of how another person thinks or the reasons behind his or her behavior. It would take many years and more than a few thousand miles of that person's life to have even a meager understanding of that person.

The fact is, even that person may not understand why he does or doesn't do a certain thing or make a specific decision. That is the reason for this book and, we hope, the reason you're reading it. As you begin to understand why you do something a certain way, eat certain kinds of food, vote for the candidates that you do, attend a specific church, temple, or mosque, you'll achieve a better grasp of why you do it. And, as you develop that understanding, you may have a better understanding of why the other person does not.

Achieving an understanding and acceptance of those ideas will make our comprehension of the topics covered in this book much easier to digest.

Along the way of answering these questions, we will discuss a topic known as Maslow's Hierarchy of Needs. We will also cover a thing called the Johari Windows. Those, combined with a sample or two of Venn diagrams, will help us grasp what goes on in each individual's mind as they wade through life.

We will also conduct exercises to explore our own thinking. These will be a little challenging for us. The intention of these exercises is to awaken us to those thought processes that we went through way back when. The processes that caused us to make a decision on how we felt about something and decided on a specific behavior.

One of our most common behaviors is that of judging others. We see someone's behavior under certain circumstances and, based on our own perceptions, judge them on what they did.

Therefore, one of the ongoing exercises we will learn is that our history of judging people, including ourselves, should be replaced by a practice of UNJUDGING people. To achieve unjudging as a practice, we must accept the fact that we simply do not know enough about the other person. As a matter of fact, we must come to realize that we still have things to learn or relearn about ourselves.

We mentioned groups a little bit ago. We must understand that groups, a collection of individuals with a semblance of agreement in certain aspects or perceptions of life, will tend to perform the same behaviors as an individual would. Because it is a group, it may seem to carry more weight than the individual. As with any mass, the larger it is, the more kinetic energy it can carry. Therefore, it may take more energy to move a group in a different direction or change its acceleration.

We will go into a bit more detail later when we discuss the various groups, religious, economic, cultural, or political, including the media and its controlled dissemination of information.

There will not be absolute statements on "right" or "wrong" behaviors. The closest to those behaviors we will get is, "lie, cheat, steal, abuse, both physical and emotional, and murder are wrong."

So often, because of the surrounding environment, we "have learned" what is right and wrong. It is only with a concerted effort that we come to understand that oftentimes, many of these rights and wrongs are merely different ways of doing things. These differences come from our local culture, which is a combination of religion, economics, government, and local customs. We will come to understand that, based on their culture, what some other folks did was perfectly okay for them.

We have also learned that some of these behaviors border on the extreme. Oftentimes, we hear the phrases "extreme right" and "extreme left." These are typically a couple of those subgroups that we mentioned earlier. While they are commonly associated with political perspectives, they may also be appropriately assigned to those same religious, economic, and cultural groups.

One of the concepts we need to understand is the sliding scale. The sliding scale consists of three parts: the top 10%, the bottom 10%, and the sliding 80% in between. These percentages are relative and flexible. We picked 10%, 10%, and 80% percent, just to give some perspective.

This might be more easily understood if we apply it to an example.

Let's say we are describing a workforce of some size, say around 100 workers. The concept says that the top 10% are the real go-getters, those who, with appropriate training, can get the job done with little or no supervision. These are the workers that, once they are working on their assigned tasks, whatever they are, should not be interrupted unless really necessary.

The bottom 10%, even though they have had all the necessary training and guidance, still seem to need constant oversight. Oftentimes, they end up being corrected on a regular basis.

Then we have the 80% in between. On a sliding scale, they range from marginally okay to very good.

And it must be understood that the range of percentages will not always represent going from the top to the bottom. In many instances, they will cover from one extreme to the other on a horizontal scale. When describing political or religious relationships, they may cover the differences from extremely liberal to extremely conservative.

We are going to use this concept throughout many of the topics we will discuss and apply it to many of the groups that we will talk about.

We talked earlier about this tricky concept called "normal." When we do this, it does not mean that something "normal" is right or wrong. At times, we may use the term to describe a point somewhere in that 80% range that we've mentioned earlier. It will pinpoint a location, a financial status, a religious perspective, or a behavior that is understood to mean what most people use as a normal behavior in a given situation.

For example, there are events in sports that cannot be construed as normal. Usain Bolt set a record in the 100-meter dash. This was an awesome accomplishment. But no one is suggesting that this is a normal, everyday behavior that most people do.

So, it must be repeated that we are not saying "right" or "wrong." We are simply saying that when this label is used, it is to maintain perspective.

We must also realize it is not other people's actions that control us. It is our reaction to their actions. We cannot control their actions, but we can control our reaction. It's also important to understand the difference between reflex and reactions. An excellent example of reflex is when the doctor taps us on the knee with the little rubber mallet. The muscle reflex causes the lower leg to jump or jerk.

When something occurs, we tend to react reflexively. If we're evaluating something that typically calls for an emotional response, and we have experienced a similar situation enough times, we might react reflexively. We react in the same way we have those other times. We may get angry, cry, feel depressed, or sad because we decided that was appropriate, may I say "right," way for that type of event.

As we said earlier, "right" is up to the person. We may not understand that person's reaction, but that does not make it wrong.

The goal of this book is to enable you to make more effective decisions in dealing with other people.

So much for our approach, now, let's talk about how we got to be the way we are.

In the Beginning, Was the Womb

One of the defining differences between men and women is the ability to give birth. Nothing in a person's experience is as life-defining as bringing a baby into the world. Biologically, this will always be the XX chromosome's neighborhood. This has restricted that experience to the female. Whether the conception was the result of a loving relationship, a forced event, such as rape, or an arranged marriage that may have little emotional involvement, the resulting birth is an event that only the female will experience.

Having said that, we must realize that giving birth is not always an eagerly anticipated event. In those instances, where incest or rape is involved, the birth may be received as a sad result of a traumatic experience.

We will discuss the impact this presents on the mother's personality later. It is mentioned here as the prelude to the beginning of an individual's personality.

There will not be any exercises in this chapter. This section is intended to give you some perspective on the very early years of life. We cover how the personality starts and why there are few, if any, memories from this life segment.

Research shows that the brain turns on in the second month following conception. At that point, the brain starts accepting input from the senses. Between weeks 16 and 18, the brain begins controlling movement and reacting to outside activity. This is the starting point of the personality.

To understand how this begins and to put this in some perspective, imagine a chalkboard that is 100,000 square feet in area. This chalkboard represents a person's personality. In the very beginning, there is nothing on that chalkboard. It is completely, totally blank.

Then, as the senses begin receiving input, starting with the sense of touch, the brain starts to respond. And, at some moment, shortly after that, a single small chalk mark appears. With that stroke of the chalk, the personality begins. As the weeks, months, and years progress, the accumulation of potentially millions of chalk marks will define a constantly developing and changing personality.

Another perspective on this first chalk mark is to consider a track-and-field event called the marathon. This is a race that covers 26 miles and 385 yards. When the starting gun goes off, every runner must take that first step. There is no way of knowing after the first step where that runner will be at the end of the race. But it must begin with that first step. And, so, it is with that first chalk mark of the personality.

From Merriam-Webster: "fetus; noun: an unborn or unhatched vertebrate especially after attaining the basic structural plan of its kind—specifically: a developing human from usually two months after conception to birth."

From this point on, the activities of the mother, her reactions to events, "good" and "bad" habits, her diet, the comfort level of her surroundings, the emotional impact of her interpersonal relationships, and the physical environment surrounding her, even the weather, will have an effect on the baby's personality before it is born. Her experiences all have a degree of emotional and sensory transmission to the fetus.

As many have read about "crack babies," those born with an already existing addiction to a specific drug, it is noted that the mother and her environment will also have an impact on the personality that is in its creative stages of development in the womb.

These events may encompass periods of peace and contentment, relaxation, moments of rest and refreshment.

These moments enable the mother's body to refresh itself and enrich its physical existence. This environment also enables the life inside to react to those same processes.

These events may also contain moments of stress, anxiety, fear, and the associated chemical actions in the mother's brain that transmit to the other regions of the body, including the fetus. And this, as mentioned previously, causes the life inside to be affected by the actions and reactions of the mother.

The recognition of this might help explain how the personality of a baby might appear in its early weeks and months following birth.

It may also explain why one baby acts and reacts very differently from another baby. The closest one baby may be to another in behavior is if they are twins or, more specifically, identical twins.

As mentioned earlier, the mind of a baby in the womb is a clean slate. As such, anything that occurs is the first time for that type of event! If things are peaceful for the mother, the baby may be relaxed, peaceful, and comfortable.

Then, something may happen to the mother. She slips or stumbles. She may catch herself by grabbing onto a piece of furniture. A worst-case situation may be that she falls to the floor. In any of these cases, she is physically jarred and shaken.

The baby feels this abruptness in movement. It knows nothing except that there was a sudden movement. There is a feeling, an awareness, possibly a reaction. At this stage, there is no reasoning yet. There is no thinking about what or why. That comes later.

The mother experiences discomfort or feels some stress because of the event. The chemistry of the mother changes. Some of that chemical reaction is passed on to the baby.

If this is a rare experience for the mother, the impact on the new life may be minimal. If circumstances are regularly peaceful, the unborn baby will remain calm.

Some parents have tried having soft, relaxing music played in the belief that the baby will have a comfortable, stress-free attitude. It's obvious, from personal experience, that relaxing music does have a calming effect on us. Therefore, it would be logical that the unborn baby would absorb that same relaxation.

The main observation in this period is that for all these weeks and months, the overriding, hoped-for environment is one of steadiness and consistency. The relative consistency that the unborn babies share means that while there are differences, the similarities will tend to override them.

While there are circumstances and structures that we have yet to cover, it is important to understand that the mother has a mental framework already in place. These emotional jungle gyms and merry-go-rounds affect her attitude and resulting behaviors, including body chemistry on a fluctuating treadmill. One of the results of her attitude and circumstances is the physical and emotional impact on the unborn baby.

While the seven-and-a-half months of awareness is comparatively short to us, it is a lifetime to the one inside. It is critical to remember that predispositions of attitude are being set.

Remember that completely clean chalkboard? Following that first chalk mark, an increase in marks will begin to accelerate at a relatively exponential rate. These marks have an intense impact at a level that will rarely, if ever, be matched later in life.

It is these impacts that begin setting aptitudes and predispositions. What constitutes the specific tendencies is unknown. What is known is that babies are different at birth. A unique brain pattern and resultant groundwork for meeting its introduction to this alien atmosphere is already present in the newborn.

All of this is just setting the stage for the epic event that starts with a shock!

After Birth Is Life

During this chapter, we will attempt to do our first recall of life's occurrences. Here, we're covering the first five years. Memories of this time frame are few and far between and vary from one person to another.

The shock of the new world is very unsettling. After all, it may have started with that smack on the bottom. It wasn't that painful. But after a lifetime of being relatively cozy and comfortable, it was a startling feeling. After being around for a few years, seven-and-a-half months doesn't seem like much.

But it constitutes a lifetime when everything is new. As time seemed to take a while when we were younger, imagine the time perception the unborn, but still alive, person felt.

Suddenly, you're in an alien universe, no longer nestled in warm fluid. Later in life, we read about going to other planets and meeting new life-forms. We've completely forgotten those first few moments when each of us was exposed to the new planet we were just thrown into. We've forgotten that these beings around us were alien life-forms at that time.

For most, the first real comfort was felt by being held in our mother's arms. The comfortable, warm, rocking feeling easily became synonymous with all that was good.

At some point, we felt a need to communicate with something or someone when we were uncomfortable. As the minutes and hours went by, we discovered that if we hollered, we got some response from these other life-forms. And, if the response didn't provide us with what we needed, we hollered some more until someone, by luck, intuition, or innate understanding, gave us what we needed.

One of the first things that irritated us was trying to sleep when all these other beings were busy doing stuff. Another irritation was waking up hungry or thirsty when there were no other beings around to feed us. Of course, we hollered 'til we got something in our tummies, whether it was food or liquid.

And as time went by, we slowly realized that these entities were people and we were connected to these people. If there were pets around, we learned that they were not the same as these entities we slowly understood to be people.

As these early weeks, months, and years passed, we were introduced to many new and unusual events. We somehow learned that there was a time and place for us to relieve ourselves when we felt discomfort down there. This appeared to bring pleasure and happiness to those wonderful people who took care of us. Then we learned to make sounds that seemed to identify certain people, and that also made them happy. As time went by, we learned to walk, learned to speak, and learned to understand basic feelings.

During this time, we began to build on some core feelings. And with these core feelings, our personality and resultant behaviors began to solidify.

At this point, we need to discuss an important topic: training.

One of the basic things to understand is that all of life is an ongoing process of learning. Learning is based on training, even though most of it is not designed as formal training.

Designed training involves something called learning objectives. With learning objectives, a lesson states specifically what the learner is going to know or be able to accomplish upon completion of the lesson.

There are, typically, three areas in the realm of training. The three areas are referred to as domains. The three domains are the cognitive, psychomotor, and affective realms. In layman's terms, that means the mental, physical, and emotional areas of activities.

Let's describe those domains a little more clearly.

The cognitive or mental domain might include remembering the dates of certain events or the steps to perform a procedure.

The psychomotor or physical domain includes things such as how to drive a nail into a piece of wood or how to strum a chord on a guitar.

Both of these domains can be quantified or translated into a numerical value to determine the successful completion of the specific task involved.

For example, in testing the mental, it may be defined as completing a task at 80% success to determine relative ability at that task. In a test that has 10 questions and the student answers eight of them correctly, that results in 80% success.

In testing the psychomotor, the student may be required to play 10 chords on a guitar. If the student plays nine of them successfully but misses one, the resulting score would be 90%.

The third domain is the affective or emotional domain. The affective domain involves how one feels about a given situation. The affective domain is unique in that it does not lend itself to a successful completion value of the topic. Trainers or teachers are unable to determine that the learner will like or appreciate a topic at a given percent on a scale. There is no way to justify saying the learner likes a subject at 75%, 80%, or 95%.

While each of these domains is important, the emotional domain has a major impact on personality. How you feel about someone or something is a critical component of your reaction and dealing with these issues or these people.

A basic understanding of these three domains may make some of the issues about learning make a little more sense as we progress through our study of personality.

While most of life does not involve specific documented lessons as we would see in a classroom environment, it must be recognized that we are continually learning every hour of every day.

In other words, we are being trained about life by experiencing life. But, always remember that while critically important, the affective domain, how we feel about the thing, will never be quantified. We will never be able to assign a specific numerical value to that feeling. We'll never know if we are at the right percentage of our understanding or appreciation of a certain thing. We won't know if our feelings about this thing give us a passing grade or not.

That brings up an interesting question. Is there such a thing as a passing grade for how we feel about an issue or a person? Forget the term "passing." Is there a correct level of "liking" something?

For that matter, are we required to have any level of liking certain things? Are there some things that we should not like?

Earlier, we mentioned that lying, cheating, stealing, or hurting someone is wrong. So, how are we supposed to learn that? Wow! This can be confusing to the completely untrained person, like a baby.

Even though there is no formal agenda during this training, there is some focus on certain specific tasks: potty training, identifying specific objects, such as rubber balls and dolls, and learning who certain people are, usually "Mommy" and "Daddy." Later on, we learned more complex procedures, one of the most famous of which was tying our shoelaces.

The hoped-for result during all of this is the satisfaction of the successful accomplishment of the task. This success is usually identified by the emotional reaction of the person attempting to get us to do whatever the job is.

Let's take a moment and look at who this person or these people are. If our caretakers, Mom and Dad, Grandma, foster parents, poor, rich, prejudiced, or religious, treated us lovingly, then we may get a warm contentment in our accomplishment.

We may accept what they say as "gospel," as fact, as natural, as normal, as "That's just the way it is."

But what if our caregivers had not been acting lovingly? What if they were short-tempered and abrupt in their attempt to get us to do the task? Hmm. Instead of a warm contentment, we may just feel a sense of relief.

What happens to us if the attitude of these seemingly colder people causes us concern, apprehension, maybe even fear?

Maybe, we would not accept what they said as fact. Maybe, as a reflex, we felt like what they said might not be right. After all, because we were not comfortable around them, we may not trust what they said.

This is where it gets a little tricky. Because these are the very early years, we haven't accumulated very many "hooks" on which to hang these events for memory purposes.

The thing to realize is that the attitude we have about our caregivers has a major impact on our perception of ourselves. This becomes a major part of our foundation, our base feeling about things around us and our position in relation to those things, including the people.

It can also have a fundamental effect on our self-confidence, our self-esteem.

We've usually read that we should learn about other cultures if we are going on a trip to a foreign country. We don't want to accidentally insult someone when traveling in another country, so we make an effort to find out how some of these alien cultures differ in their habits from the habits we learned in our culture.

We must realize that for a newborn baby, our culture is alien to them. The baby knows nothing about correct behaviors or incorrect behaviors.

One of the first things to be aware of is who is or are the primary caregiver(s) of the child. For most babies, this is the mother and father. But for many, there are a lot of other possibilities. Because of various circumstances, these caregivers may be grandparents or aunts and uncles. It might be just the mother or just the father, a single grandparent or aunt or uncle. In some instances, there may not be a near relative and the baby may end up being adopted or be sent into foster care. Every one of these possibilities will change the effect of the relationship between the caregiver and the baby. And these situations will all have an effect on how the baby's perceptions of people change.

Another issue that affects these relationships is the interactions that occur between the adult caregivers. How well do the mother and father, or the grandparents, or the aunt and uncle get along with each other? That relationship will have an impact on how the baby or very young child begins to perceive relationships.

There are also potentially caustic situations: single mom or dad, alcoholic mom or dad, abusive mom or dad, divorced mom or dad, widowed mom or dad, cheating mom or dad, etc.

And, of course, there are differences based on the relationship between the baby and other siblings, brothers and/or sisters. The firstborn, the oldest, will act differently than the others. They may be put in charge of the others at a certain age. Therefore, the baby will have to figure out how these relationships differ.

All of these scenarios are part of this baby's normal. Each one of these has a modifying impact on each child. Each colors the perception of what constitutes appropriate behavior in given situations. Because the circumstances differ from baby to baby, this is just one aspect of how a very young personality will continue to differ from other very young personalities.

Take a moment and try to remember the last time that something really made you sit up and take notice. Something struck you as being out of the ordinary. Something that made you think about what just happened and why.

To a baby, this will happen at least once or twice or maybe several times a day. Starting without any history and then progressing to very little history, so much is still very unusual in this strange land.

Babies have a very short attention span, and because the slate is still relatively clean, most things have a strong, however brief, impression. The priorities focus on the attempts to gain control over the environment, such as dealing with an empty tummy or adjusting to a sudden chill or excessive warmth under a blanket.

Another important topic that we will discuss briefly is prejudice. This is an umbrella term that covers many groups. It is doubtful that any group is free from prejudice. It is also important to realize that every one of us belongs to more than one group, whether we intend to "join" them or not. Every one of us was born a male or a female. We are either black, white,

Asian, or some more specific ethnicity. You, I, and everyone else is taught or developed some form of a moral or ethical standard, whether it's based on an established religion or some culturally conceived form of right and wrong.

Those are just four of the myriad groups available. We are in these simply by our birth and resulting life. And each one is susceptible to prejudice. We may have been told that some of this is referred to as stereotyping and that it is intended as an instinctive method of protecting ourselves from the "others," those from a different clan, religion, race, or country.

Let's take a look at the commonality of these differences. We mentioned the term "culture" earlier. What do we mean when we use this word?

Culture is the collection of behaviors based on the attitudes and beliefs of a group that we see, hear, and read about.

Because a culture is made up of individuals, there will be a wide variety of these behaviors that occur within specific groups.

For example, there is no white culture, just as there is no black culture. There are different white cultures and different black cultures. There are cultures that include some blacks and some whites.

Because there are these differences, we have the concept of prejudice. Prejudice is the prejudging of people and groups. In other words, we tend to prejudge other people and groups. That prejudging results in our differences in behavior when we are involved with folks from those in the prejudged group.

Prejudging is based on the basic human instinct to protect our group from other groups. The most common prejudices are racial, religious, political, and national.

Prejudice is typically based on lack of knowledge.

Problems arise when we carry this "protection" into our relationships with the proverbial "blinders" in the on position. We use this stereotyping in a manner that forces us to treat people as one of the others without applying any attempt at understanding the person as anything other than the defined description we learned earlier in life.

But this is not a book about sociology or group behavior. It is about understanding how these outside behaviors impact one's perception of life and appropriate personal behavior.

Within every group are people who think a little differently. It's that little difference that breaks the groups that frustrate the "leaders" of these groups.

At this point, we need to recognize some of the obvious groupings that occur in life. These groupings have an overriding impact on a person's personality. As with all groupings, the individual can alter the impact on their personality. However, the cultural-economic aspects of these groupings will produce the inherent pressure associated with them.

Some common examples of these groupings are the religious, political, financial, and educational categories. Every one of these, in varying degrees, pressures the person to behave in certain ways.

Being raised in a secular household can be subtly but distinctly different from a religious one. Not being able to go out and play 'til you've returned from Sunday school or other church services, only to see some of your other friends already out and about at the playground or riding around on their bicycles, will give you a different perspective.

One of the things in growing up is an item called childhood or infantile amnesia. While not a hard and fast rule, it basically says that we tend not to remember things that occurred during the first three to five years.

This says that it is possible to learn something and not remember learning it. This can cause serious problems later because you can easily think everyone should "just know this."

Exercise 4-1

Take a minute and think about your earliest years. Try to recall some of those events. Perhaps it was a birthday party or a holiday celebration.

There might be memories of being disciplined for doing something wrong. Perhaps you had an accident or saw someone else have an accident.

Spend some time trying to recall any of these early events, regardless of the relative importance of the occasion. What about those that you remember? Why do you think you remember these occasions and not others? Was there anything in particular about any one of these memories that sticks out in your mind?

Okay! We got through the first five years. A lot has happened to us already. As mentioned earlier, some predispositions have been set, possibly including some prejudices. We have experienced some "warm fuzzies" about some of the folks around us and, perhaps, a few concerns about some of the others. We know that some of these people are called family, while others are called friends.

It's important to remember that prejudice is the normal attitude of all people. It mainly consists of stereotypes that include everyone who is different from you or your family, your clan, your tribe, your race, or your religion. It's also important to remember that there is no white, black, or Asian culture. The fact is, there are several of each. Whether it's race, religion, political leaning, or any of the other groups, there are several cultures in each of these groups. Remember that all prejudice is based on a lack of knowledge about those groups. We will learn how to develop that knowledge as we go through life.

But, at this point, we've learned a foreign language and experienced some acrobatic feats, including walking, sitting up, and rolling over. We developed an understanding of and are pretty accomplished at handling these eating tools known as forks and spoons, bowls, and glasses. Oh, and straws, those were fun.

All in all, we kind of feel pretty good about ourselves. However, for some of us, we might not have that same sense of comfort because our caretakers, people we know are in control of us, don't tell us how good we are. So, we may not be as sure of ourselves as we would like.

Somewhere around this time, we are taken away to this place called school. We're told that we're going to kindergarten and will be with a lot of other people about our age that we'll get to play with.

These early years set a lot of attitudes and impressions. They contain many of our general outlooks on life and people. They tend to create the base set of our philosophy about life, people, and groups.

Because our slate is still relatively bare of memories, the learning that occurs is not clouded by that much previous baggage. Since we are still experiencing many things as new, we basically accept these things as natural. They become our normal.

Wow! Our normal! What does our normal mean?

We must step back and envision those times, those environments, those types of cultures. History did not start the day we were born. Each of us is simply the latest in generations of births and deaths and a prelude to the next in an ongoing sequence. When we read or hear about how bad crime is, how crooked politicians are, how terrible some of the pastors, priests, rabbis, or imams are, we ignore the fact that this is nothing new in history.

We're still too young to have a grasp of history. We've just gotten a grasp of being alive.

Was That a Nudge or a Shove?

And so we begin a new form of life experience. We'll have more work to do in facing the memories we have. We are more capable of retaining memories, so we'll have a much larger volume of material to wade through.

We start this second kind of routine that has us going to this place called school on a regular basis. As we start to go through this outside life, new things happen around us. Each of these things has an effect on us. These effects range from subtle to traumatic. We'll refer to the subtle ones as nudges.

The nudges have a minimal, sometimes very indistinct, effect on us. The traumatic happenings we'll call shoves. Shoves jolt us, just as someone physically shoving us would do.

Now, the nudges and shoves started much earlier, actually starting in the womb. We are introducing the concept now because this point in life is the first major shift in what we consider a common process in life. And it's at this point we can understand and relate to their occurrence.

These nudges and shoves occur regularly every day. Experience indicates that we receive hundreds of nudges every day. Since the nudges and shoves vary in intensity, the crossover events going from a nudge to a shove is a gray area.

On other occasions, the stimuli are not subtle but jarring in their force. We refer to these times as shoves. These are the moments we may bring up in conversation with friends or family members. We interject them as, "Did I tell you about…" or "You won't believe what happened when…." They range from somewhat memorable all the way to traumatic.

The shoves are not gentle or peaceful but rather jarring, even shocking. If they reach the traumatic level, they may not only extremely reinforce our perception of something or someone, they may even cause our feelings on a subject to completely reverse itself. They have the potential to make us do a U-turn about something, causing us to go from loving to hating, from caring to disdainful.

Some early shoves cross a border and enter into the realm of trauma. Being beaten or molested during the early years is an example of this. Even if the memories of these events are suppressed, their impact on the child's feelings and later behaviors may be indelible.

Observing others' behaviors can also be categorized as traumatic. Having a parent who is an alcoholic will leave its mark on our psyche. Watching the mother or father drink excessively and pass out or cause damage to their surroundings will impact the child's feelings and perceptions of right or wrong behaviors.

Most of us learn the same things, but we learn them at different points or ages in our lives. Learning about something may be a goal. The process of active learning should be a goal. Someone may learn something at 16 while someone else learns the same thing, but not until they are 60.

We receive stimuli from the things our senses perceive every day in our lives. We see, hear, smell, touch, and taste all manner of things. Each of these things affects us in one way or another. Hearing a few bars of a certain tune may bring back memories of a pleasant time. Tasting something bitter may cause us momentary irritation.

All of these events not only cause a certain reaction, but they may also detract from or reinforce our feelings about something or someone.

Somewhere, we become predisposed to certain issues. For example, let's suppose that the first time we tasted ice cream, it was vanilla. It tasted so good that we decided we really liked vanilla ice cream. After that, if anyone asked us what flavor of ice cream we liked, we'd say vanilla. We didn't even think about another flavor because vanilla tasted so good. We just couldn't imagine anything else tasting that good.

That is how predispositions start. On the following occasions when ice cream was an option, we just said we liked vanilla. It became what we refer to as a reflexive response. We didn't put any thought into it, we just knew that vanilla was the right answer.

Now, the first time that we had vanilla would be considered a shove. It was a relatively major event. It was our first time with ice cream; it happened to be vanilla. It tasted so good that we connected the vanilla flavor with ice cream, and that was that.

Shoves are just that. They have a major impact on our feelings about a topic. In the early years, they are related to the first time of being involved with a specific item or issue.

Another example of a shove might be that after so many years of vanilla ice cream, we tried rocky road. Wow! This is so very, very good, it just puts vanilla out of the picture! We thought vanilla was it for so many years that we couldn't believe it could be replaced. But here we are with rocky road! We just experienced another shove on a specific issue!

A real-life shove may create a new normal. The ice cream example helps to clarify what we mean by a shove, but a more serious one may be the loss of a parent, the loss of a child, or the loss of a loved one. It might also be the loss of a job or a contract for a job. Obviously, events such as divorces or bankruptcies would qualify as shoves.

Shoves don't necessarily involve a specific action on our part, like eating a certain food, but might be the result of hearing something being discussed by others, oftentimes adults. We may hear another group referred to by a rude name. It might be the first time we heard about this group as a specific collection of folks, and the name, while flattering or unflattering, sticks in our mind as the name for that group.

Then, we have the shove designed as a nudge. This is a deceptive event in that it appears as a casual statement. Someone makes a seemingly inoffensive comment that includes a label about a group that sticks in your mind. Without thinking about it, you begin using that label to identify individuals in that group.

Sometimes, the timing of an event alters the reaction. It may change from a nudge to a shove or the reverse, a shove to a nudge. If you had just received a shove and then received another shove, the second one may come as just a nudge.

As we mentioned earlier, one of the first shoves is starting school. This may be kindergarten, or, for many nowadays, the shove may have occurred in preschool. The shove may involve the shock of being in a strange place with a bunch of strange people our age and two or more adults who seemed to be running things. These adults would tell us what to do. That took some getting used to.

That first day of school would be considered a shove. By the second or third day, going to school would be relegated to a repetitive nudge.

After kindergarten, we continued on with school, spending what seemed like forever going from one grade to another with a nice but altogether too brief break during the summers.

There was always the stress of having to be successful in school. If we were, there was the relief that made us a little more comfortable with ourselves. If we were not as successful as we would like, or as our mommy and daddy would like, then there might be the sense of not being as worthy as we would like to be.

For many, it had an impact on our feelings of worthiness compared to the other students. For most, we were better than some and worse than some. And for many, this impacted our confidence level in relation to the other students. This, in turn, had an effect on how we related to the other students. We could easily fall into the trap of thinking that if we were better in school, then we would be smarter, more capable, or better. With that type of thinking, our reaction to events might tend to be more cautious.

We should bring up another set of terms that are commonly used. Those are "ignorant" and "stupid." For the discussions in this book, we are going to use the following definitions.

Ignorance means we do not know certain information. For example, I might be ignorant of electricity. Someone else might be ignorant of quantum physics. No one knows everything. Therefore, everyone is ignorant of several things. There is nothing wrong with being ignorant of something.

Stupid means someone has been trained about something or shown how to perform a certain procedure, but still does the procedure incorrectly. For example, let's say I have received training about changing an electrical outlet. When I replaced the electrical outlet, I did something that I was told not to do. After receiving a suitable electrical shock after doing the no-no, I could safely be told that I was stupid.

With this seemingly endless series of nudges and shoves, we are able to describe some of the scheduled shoves that life has planned for us. These are based on customs, laws, and psychological or religious practices. Let's take a look at these and get an understanding of what the factors are.

The issue to keep in mind through this trip down life's timeline is the impact that occurs on our personality and resultant behavior.

Let's take a few minutes and look at some of the specific points in life where shoves occur based on our passage through life.

As you review each of these life points, take a moment and recall when you experienced or passed through that particular time. Recall a memory that sticks out in your mind that was relative to that point. Why do you think you recall that event? Was it a positive or negative memory? Did it modify my attitude?

Age of reason

Around the age of 11 or 12, we enter the stage referred to as the age of reason. We had spent the previous years asking questions and usually accepting what the person we were asking said.

The age of reason, however, flipped a switch in our mind. While we still asked questions, we started trying to answer them ourselves. The questions usually started with "Why." "Why did some classmates laugh at my joke and the others did not?" "Why did he/she say or do that?"

Teen years

Ahh! The glorious years of being a teenager, that seven year stretch following the age of reason when we seem to lose all sense of that new skill! At least, that is what our parents or other adults tell us.

Nonetheless, the chemical and biological changes occurring in the body create a tumultuous, emotional roller coaster. Maintaining our cool during this period is difficult, to say the least. All of our predispositions in our attitudes, habits, and relationships are shaken. Just as an example, if we have been religious, we may become an atheist, or if an atheist, we may become religious.

We can't believe adults are so clueless. They just don't understand that life is different from when they were our age, which, obviously, was ages ago for them.

Driver's license

Usually, this is our first taste of what we consider freedom. We also realize that there is some level of responsibility that we face from forces outside of our parents, caretakers, or teachers.

Breaking the law

The age of occurrence varies, but most have done this. Usually, it's breaking the speed limit when driving. But, it may have been something more serious.

Draft

The military draft requirements change as the years go by. But, when in force, they require men to register when they reach the age of 18. Having women register has never yet been part of the draft requirements.

College or trade school

For those who attend one or the other, this is another event that brings its own level of stress. While the environment is very different from high school, it still brings its unique form of concern.

Voting

Becoming eligible to vote does not necessarily contain much in the way of pressure, it is another hallmark of aging.

Marriage

Ahh! Marriage! For many, this is the first time we make a major decision that we realize requires a major shift in our outlook on not only our personal behavior but also another person's attitudes and actions.

Children

Wow! If life hasn't gotten your attention yet, this should do it.

At this point, we're going to discuss a topic referred to as Maslow's Hierarchy of Needs. Refer to Figure 4-1 for this description. Abraham Maslow was a psychologist born on April

1, 1908. His concept of "needs" described a structure of human needs that had an impact on behaviors.

Figure 4-1

The basic needs consisted of "food on the table, roof over your heads, and clothes on your back."

To emphasize this perspective, an iPad, a new TV, or a cell phone are not needed. Things such as these are wants. While the wants list may be short or long, it is important to accept the difference between needs and wants.

While the above needs may have been recognized in early adulthood or marriage, they will inevitably be accepted upon the arrival of children. At this point, those basic requirements of successfully moving forward will apply to one's activities.

If there are problems achieving these needs, they will impact one's thinking and resultant attitude and behavior. Whether it is getting and keeping a job, moving onward and upward in career, realizing what the limits are in one's spending, meeting critical challenges as they arise, such as medical issues, our behaviors are nudged and shoved.

Decision-making involves two factors, both cognitive and effective: thinking and feeling. If we make a decision based only on how we feel, we may take an action that could be considered rash. If we make the decision only on thinking, it may be considered cold or heartless. Therefore, most decisions are a combination of both elements.

Divorce

This is another life event that can have a strong effect on one's daily attitude and activity. The uncomfortable scenario of a relationship crumbling is always disturbing. The associated blames and recriminations, the degree of difficulty in determining one's level of responsibility in the breakup, the distribution of financial and physical assets, all contribute to levels of stress.

Jobs and career

Becoming part of the workforce and eventually settling on and working one's way through a career path will carry unique facets of stresses and rewards.

Insurance

Seemingly as important as Maslow's survival needs are those dealing with insurance coverage, both life and medical. Both of these deal with the fundamental gambling against "what ifs." We don't want to face a "what if," but we know that we have to have a plan just in case.

Savings

Some do this very naturally and easily. It becomes as regular as getting up in the morning. For others of us, it's one of those things that we will get around to doing one of these days.

Grandchildren

Welcoming the first grandchild brings some sense of accomplishment, even though we didn't really have anything to do with its occurrence.

Approaching retirement

We wake one day and realize, "Wow!" Have I been getting ready for this properly? Have I been saving enough? Is my company stable and ready to support its pension plan?

What's the "full retirement age" now for Social Security?

Retirement

Well, I gave my notice. Friday is actually the last day. Folks have been stopping by and wishing me well, asking if I'm ready to go fishing or shopping or taking that trip I've been talking about.

Early retirement years

This is nice. Better than I expected. Time for the grandkids to come visit again. Or, I can't take sitting around anymore. I need to do something. Maybe I'll see about being a Walmart greeter and receipt checker.

Later retirement years

Health issues seem to be the topic of just about every discussion. Who has what conditions, and who has had what surgeries? What is very interesting is the differences in attitudes of the individuals.

Last years

Life is not through with you yet. But, unless something unusual arises, you are at a point where life has settled into some semblance of a routine. Few things are a surprise anymore. You've experienced much, and you know that each day is fairly consistent or repetitive with the previous. Your personality has become relatively stable. You've seen and experienced a lot. Shoves have pretty much disappeared, and nudges are very subtle at this point.

Death of Spouse

Ah, shoves did not completely disappear. For many, life seems to have lost a lot of purpose. For some, it's the end of a relationship that may have started in high school. While the intensity of the loss varies from couple to couple, the length of the relationship has a determining factor on the depth of the loss. The longer the time spent sharing life increases the agony of that loss.

While some of these do not have specific ages or dates in life, they are all indelible occurrences. Not everyone experiences all of these. Some remain single all their lives. Some do not have children. Not everyone goes on to college or trade school. But you can see how each of these events has an impact on our perception of life and our behaviors. And, as stated several times, they affect our personalities.

Gentle though they are, it is important to recognize the total impact of these events. As the years go by, these accumulated nudges and shoves reinforce our feelings, attitudes, and opinions about many aspects of life. After a portion of our life has passed, we consider our opinions to be so blatantly obvious that we consider any other opinions to border on absurd.

One of the traps that many of us fall into is that of the echo chamber. The echo chamber is a seductive process. We hear something that we agree with, and it reinforces our previously held feelings. If we don't agree with it, we tend to ignore it as a foolish opinion and ignore it. The trap aspect of it is that we don't stop and think, "Gee, is there something here that I should investigate further?" Life changes, events back then may not be the same as events now. We quit questioning things like we used to do. We think we've already learned about this and stop learning anymore.

Let's take a moment and talk about three groups of achievement: the top 10%, the bottom 10%, and the 80% in between. The numerical values 10, 10, and 80 are not fixed but flexible and are simply used to develop a perception of possibilities.

In any group of appreciable size, there always appears to be a group at the top, in our discussion the first 10%. In the workplace, there are those who appear to develop an understanding of the assigned tasks very easily. Once they've been shown how to perform the job, they start performing the procedure very effectively and require little, if any supervision.

At the other end, we have seen those who, even after they've been shown how to do the job, seem to continually have questions about one or more of the required steps to get the task done. They continually make mistakes and just never seem to understand what has to be done.

In between the top and bottom, we have the 80% that range from marginally acceptable to very good.

In every function in life, we see individuals from these three groups as they go through the routines in life.

Of course, no one is necessarily locked into one of these groups automatically or forever. Just as the percentages are flexible, so are the participants in the groups.

Another thing to consider is the physics of relationships. So, what does physics have to do with relationships? Imagine a small car with a suitably small engine. The car runs satisfactorily as designed with the engine. Now, imagine that engine being put into a much larger car. Well, it's not going to run as effectively. It certainly won't have the acceleration that it did with the small car. It won't be as smooth getting around in traffic.

The same thing happens in relationships. If you're having a discussion with another person in a one-on-one conversation, things may go along fairly smoothly. You may disagree on the topic under discussion, and one of you may persuade the other to change their opinion. Even if neither of you changes your position, it still may go fairly smoothly and end comfortably.

Now, imagine that it's just you, but there are two or three others who disagree and are involved in the discussion. The chances of you persuading the other side to change your perspective drop noticeably. Where one may begin to have doubts about their stance, another will kick in with a different detail on the issue, causing the one who had doubts to stay firm in the position with the additional reinforcement.

The increased size of the other side, with the additional input they provide, may even begin to cause you to have doubts about your perspective.

In physics, it is the increases in mass, more than one or two times, that increase the power of that side.

With respect to your thinking, the event of the discussion may end up being a nominal nudge to even a shove.

While the nudges and shoves occur regularly throughout life, there are times when shoves will occur at specific ages or events. We will identify them as life points. They are easily identified by age or event.

We just covered the first block of events, the first few years of school. And, because we are still early in life, time moves somewhat slowly. A school year takes soooo loooong. And our accomplishments in school appear to define how good we are. Our self-confidence feels so dependent on our success in school.

One example of the complexity of predispositions is that of twin brothers. The father was an alcoholic. Later in life, one of the brothers became an alcoholic, while the other never touched a drop. When asked about it, the alcoholic son said that he became a drinker because of his father, while the other said he would never touch alcohol because of his father. Why the difference between the two? Somewhere, somehow, the sequence of life events affected each of the brothers differently.

Something occurred sometime earlier that made their perception of their dad different. Oftentimes, these "somethings" are forgotten. They happened, they made the effects, and they became buried in memory. They were isolated instances, one for one of the brothers and another for the other. For as often as the twins were together, there were times when they were not. Therefore, each has seen something that the other did not. And a difference in perception occurred.

Earlier, we talked about things going on behind closed doors. At this point, we need to recognize and cover some of the things that occur in public. These include religious affiliation, economic status, political leanings of the family, and surrounding culture.

How the family deals with their religion is understood to be its normal. If the family goes to a church, synagogue, mosque, or temple on a regular basis, the beliefs and associated practices become part of the regular behaviors.

To get some perspective on these, we'll try an exercise. The exercise will take us through parts of the day. The focus of the exercise requires you to evaluate what you're doing and why.

Let's take a pause here and consider what we've learned.

Every individual experiences constant adjustments during their life through numerous nudges and shoves. Oftentimes, they ask themselves, "What if he/she/I did it differently?" Or, "Why did I say that?"

Sometimes, they recognize that knowledge without emotional content is not really knowledge. Unless a person experiences the emotional content of a situation, true learning does not occur.

With the commonality of certain points in life, we've discovered that seemingly trivial things can result in differences in our responses to these events. While many predispositions were set in the early years, the nudges and shoves that we received and will continue to receive for the rest of our lives, will continue to mold our perceptions and resultant behaviors as our personality maintains its constant development and refinement.

Exercise 5-1

This exercise is to clarify your understanding of Maslow's Hierarchy of Needs.

Think about your attempts to provide the basics for yourself and/or your family. Are you able to provide these basics successfully?

When it's time to get the groceries, have you ever had to count the pennies? Did you have to use coupons to save money or because you have to just so you can afford what you need?

Does paying the rent or mortgage payment cause you concern? How about the utilities?

The point of this exercise is not how successful you are financially but how the degree of ease or difficulty impacts your attitude. If providing the basics causes you some level of distress, this rolls over into your comfort with just getting through the day. If it increases your level of stress, it can easily bleed over into your ability to deal with coworkers and customers.

Exercise 5-2

Play devil's advocate (reflexively disagree). Even if you agree, it helps to make your brain work. One of the activities in high school is debate class. The primary function of debate class is to be able to defend either side of a response to a question.

This requires studying the question and gaining enough information about what the possible responses might result in.

By playing devil's advocate, you are automatically forcing the other person to defend their statement, their viewpoint.

Obviously, you will want to do this in a tactful, respectful manner. You might initiate the talk with the phrase, "Just for discussion, I would suggest that...," and then make your statement which offers an alternative to theirs.

It's important to remember that there are no intended winners or losers in the process. The purpose is to expand your learning to accept that there are alternatives to suggested actions.

Exercise 5-3

Make three lists:

1) Things you like about your life.

2) Things you do not like about your life.

3) Things you would like to do but wouldn't or couldn't.

Explain the reasons behind each one.

Saints and Sinners, Geniuses and Idiots

So far, we've been looking at how our personalities have developed based on internal reactions to relatively normal outside events; we're going to explore some of the more extreme individuals and groups and how their actions impact our perceptions of events. To do this, we're going to use the terms saints and sinners, and geniuses and idiots.

When we use these terms, saints and sinners, geniuses and idiots, we are not referring to any specific religion or belief system, nor are we referring to any standardized categories based on general-purpose, intelligence-testing results. For saints and sinners, we are using these words as they are commonly understood to refer to particularly good or very bad individuals. For geniuses and idiots, we will talk about folks who appear to be very sharp and those who are just not very swift.

Before we get into these groupings, let's pause and check on a "normal." Now, we know normals come in a lot of different flavors, so this is simply a typical view.

We must include a quick side note. There are places in the world where, because of lack of resources or government or economic structure, people are struggling to meet that first level on the hierarchy of needs. Also, there always seems to be a war or revolutionary action going on someplace in the world.

Those folks are suffering through a lot of shoves. Their normal is vastly different from most other normals.

The average person anywhere in the world wants to wake up in the morning, go to work, produce something, go home, have dinner, spend time with the family and spouse, go to sleep, wake up the next morning, and do it all over again. In the interim, they expect some time for entertainment, other enjoyable time with the family, and some version of holidays.

In other words, we all have very similar, basic routines, while we are still as different as we could possibly be. Therefore, for the purposes of this book, all observations, unless otherwise defined, are based on the presumption that we are peers. But what is a peer?

In a court of law in many modern countries, we have decided that we will be judged by a jury of our peers. Now, a peer is supposed to be someone as much like us as is reasonably possible without actually being us. We might go so far as to say a peer is the same as our normal under specific circumstances.

So, who qualifies as a peer? Lawyers, that amazing group of people who have been trained to prove that green is pink and one minute later prove that "No, green is actually blue," sometimes spend hours selecting who our peers are.

The end result, we hope, is that they have selected the most unbiased group of people that could exist for the reason they are there, specifically to judge our existence at the event under question and, if so, judge our behavior at that event. Yes, we know that the lawyer's goal is to get the type of folks they want on that jury, whether it's the prosecutor or the defense lawyer. We're not going to get into all the psychological tactics on this issue.

The whole point of this part of the discussion is to establish a baseline of understanding about people, our coworkers, people who support the same professional sports team that we do, people who agree with us politically or religiously or don't. This part of talking is to make us realize that we are very much the same as many others while maintaining our very distinct personalities.

Let's first discuss the saints. We've met people throughout our lives who seem to always be kind and gentle in their demeanor. They never make remarks about others that in any way sound like a put-down or diminish any individual in that way.

They may attend some form of religious service on a regular basis. Oftentimes, they may volunteer their time in various charitable functions, such as assisting the poor or visiting penal institutions to provide some counseling to inmates. The point being that these folks tend to do things that are helpful to others.

Then we have the sinners. We have probably met them. If we read or watch any news, we are aware of them. We see or hear them as they insult others either in the workplace or just talk about others in one or more of the other groups in a demeaning manner. We may read about them accosting others. We learn from the news about them perpetrating fraud or, sadly, murdering someone.

Next up are the geniuses. These folks always get good grades, better jobs, and promotions. Their families have good interpersonal relationships, with divorce being a rare event.

And, finally, the idiots. They're not necessarily dumb, but they just seem to miss getting a good raise or a promotion. In school, they always get mediocre, if not poor, grades. Incentives don't seem to be one of their traits.

Now, the big step. With a little honest thinking, we should realize that each of us has been one of these, saint, sinner, genius, or idiot, at one or more times in our life. We've done good things and helped others. We've done wrong things, told white lies, fudged on taxes, or exceeded the speed limits. We've studied and excelled on a test in school or presented a great idea on the job. We ignored a safety precaution and injured ourselves, or didn't pay attention in class and flunked a test.

So, what kind of reaction do you have when associating with these types of people? Does being around someone who is acting nicely irritate you or make you feel comfortable when in their company? When someone makes an insulting remark about another group, do you add another insulting remark about that group, remain silent, or attempt to correct that person's statement?

When a coworker comes up with an idea that will improve the performance of a job, do you feel jealous or compliment them on their great idea? If another driver cuts in front of you, do you use a colorful expression about their intelligence, or do you realize you've done the same thing before and continue driving peacefully?

You make these choices pretty much every day. The choices you make are a result of your thinking and, at the same time, reinforce or modify your thinking.

Above all, remember, you can disagree with someone and you can both be right!

Stories have been written over the centuries about characters performing certain acts, treating others in certain ways, seeming to have little or no feelings for the concerns of others. Because these characters are fictitious, it may seem that they represent people who would never really exist. But, the hard-to-accept fact is, those characters not only represent real people, it's the real people who exhibit much, much worse behaviors than the characters we read about.

No one is or has been perfect. Every "hero/heroine" in every culture has done things that would be considered bad. Every saint was a sinner.

As always, these are not intended to reflect any of the groups that a person may belong to.

With that in mind, we say that in every group of appreciable size, for example, sizes exceeding a hundred people, there is a percentage of saints and sinners. The group may be black, white, Asian, Baptist, Catholic, Buddhist, Muslim, male, female, conservative, liberal, independent, French, Chinese, Zimbabwean, Indian, German, etc. And they all have a percentage of these four categories.

Now, the reflex that many of us have is, "Yeah, but there are more sinners (or idiots) among the...," opposite group, whichever it may be. This is a normal reaction among most folks. It is typical of the "echo chamber" perspective that many of us fall prey to when reading articles or listening to news programs or video clips. And, as suggested earlier, we must practice the unjudging effort on groups as well as individuals.

So, the first thing we need to do is come to an understanding. With all the books written about psychology, sociology, religion, philosophy, human behavior, and any or all variations of those terms, there is one very fundamental baseline that is expressed in all of them. The thing is that with all the variables, prejudices, beliefs, and cultural norms that we recognize as existing within each of us, we must agree that there is such a thing as the basic person.

So, how do we decide what might be a "normal" or basic human being? Do we use how most people voted in the last few elections? Do we use the group making up the highest percentage of the "local" population? Should we restrict it to one category? If we feel we have to use two, three, or more categories to determine normal, then what categories should we consider and what percent or weight do we give each of these groups?

The point at issue is each of us, as individuals, must agree that, with minor variations, all groups are made up of a common percentage of types within each of the groups being discussed.

That being said, there are some blatantly obvious differences. If we were to discuss terrorists, for example, we are talking about people who are out to do grievous bodily harm to other people simply because there is a disagreement about a fundamental concern of the group wanting to do harm. So, if we are discussing the saints in that group, we are obviously looking at a select group of folks whose perspective will be different from what would be considered normal to the vast majority of humanity.

In between the saints and sinners and the geniuses and idiots, there is a sliding scale containing everyone in between these sets of extremes.

Now it's time to talk about the groups. As with individuals, we have to understand that groups can also be identified as saints, sinners, geniuses, and idiots. And they carry the same combinations as the individuals.

We also have to understand that groups have a common agreement about a specific issue. The group is a collection of individuals who have joined together for a defined purpose. It could be something very simple, such as getting together on a regular basis for a function such as a bridge club party. The fact that they identify themselves as a specific group means that they represent a specific agenda or purpose for practicing or representing a certain commonality.

While many groups are relatively harmless and are intended to provide pleasure and enjoyment, others have a more sinister agenda. For example, there are groups that have been referred to as "fifth columns." A fifth column is an internal group that acts as an enemy to a larger group. In wartime, it's thought of as a group that acts against the country in which it exists. So, to that country, it would be considered an enemy or a sinner group. But, obviously, to the enemy of the country, it would be considered a saintly group. These are perceptions based on relationships.

Other groups would include religions, political parties, governments, and media, such as TV and radio stations, internet sites, or corporations. And, of course, there are smaller groups such as cities, neighborhoods, local churches, all the way down to families.

Each of these groups has an impact on us. If we're property owners and pay property taxes, we may complain about how the city is run, whether they're collecting trash or maintaining the roads properly.

Are our neighbors friendly and sociable, or is the area having a problem with gangs?

Do our family members get along? Or do we have a problem with Uncle Joe or Cousin Susan? Are our parents loving and considerate, but the son or daughter is regularly disrespectful or hateful in their language? Or is it reversed with loving children and mean parents?

All of these group relationships have an impact on our feelings, personality, and resultant behavior.

Exercise 6-1

This may be an uncomfortable exercise for some of us. We're either a parent or a child. Some of us may be both. If we're both, we'll have to go through this exercise twice, once for each position.

As a child, recall your relationship with each of your parents or caregivers. Select an event that was stressful in an uncomfortable way. At the time of this event, what caused the stress? What was your reaction? What was your parent's reaction? Did it cause a change in your behavior? Why?

Repeat the exercise if you are the parent.

One of the noteworthy groups in our discussion is the media, more specifically, the written books and/or news media. In modern use, this group is known as the fourth estate. In America, the freedom of the press has enabled this group to operate relatively freely.

The extreme behaviors of the other groups are those who usually make the news in the media, the fourth estate. They are those that the media focuses on when they give their presentations of the news and editorials.

The organizations that represent the media have all this information available to them and decide which items they are going to present. The directors of these organizations themselves have their perceptions, including their biases. Embedded with these biases, they have a specific audience that they perform for. And, behind all of this is the money. Nothing's free, and the money is an investment for profit. While many organizations depend on advertising to generate the income that pays everyone's salaries, there has to be an initial investment that starts and supports this.

Depending on which group you may closely associate with, it may appear to you that some of the media have crossed the line in delivering a balanced presentation of the news. Some folks think that parts of the Fourth Estate have become a fifth column in its position and presentation.

The saints and sinners also come in groups. Some of the groups include the radio and TV news media, the entertainment industry, with movies, TV series, and live shows and concerts, and newspapers, both printed and online.

Many folks have expressed concerns about the appropriateness of some television series and the content that is available for the younger generations. Others have been dismayed at the content of song lyrics. And others have felt that the free press has undermined traditional attitudes about the health of the country.

Some folks feel that the old phrase, "If it bleeds, it leads," has been replaced by, "If it skews, it's news."

Exercise 6-2

Pick one of the news media's presentations. Is it typically one that you go to not only for news but also for opinion pieces?

Now, do an evaluation of the one you selected. Is it one that you usually agree with? If it is, do you go to other channels, books, or radio stations that you tend to disagree with? If you typically go to other sources as well as your first preference, you may be practicing open-minded thinking. If you don't normally go to other sources, you may be falling into the trap of the echo chamber.

As mentioned earlier, commonly using the echo chamber will tend to close your mind to other ways of thinking. Again, remember there are a lot more differences than there are rights and wrongs.

All of these groups have had a collective impact on group perceptions and resulting individual behaviors.

It must be understood that these saints and sinners, geniuses, and idiots do not necessarily define their group. If their behavior toward a specific incident is based on the predominant point of the group, then it might well be a defining incident. If it is a balanced presentation, then it would be considered neutral.

Oftentimes, some are guilty of purposely taking this incident as being typical of the group or of someone in the given group. This will also be a mistake.

It should be understood that news is a product. It has its market share and its market. Just like some people prefer Fords over Chevys, they prefer CNN over FOX. Like any other product, news agencies have their niche of readers and viewers who are selective in their bias. For the independents or those truly looking for an unbiased perspective, try the Associated Press, Reuters, or some others.

Earlier, we mentioned the sliding scale of groups. Let's apply that concept here.

First, we have the top 10%. They are generally very good people. They rarely say anything derogatory about people. They are pleasant and reliable workers.

Then there are the 10% who are not very nice. It is not unusual for them to make statements critical of coworkers. Because of a grouchy attitude, they are not comfortable to work around.

And, in between, are the 80% on a sliding scale ranging from being occasionally irritable to usually being very nice.

Of course, it must be restated that these percentages are variable and are based on large groups of 100 or more people.

Governments, to the best of their ability, try to ensure that we have achieved that first level. Additionally, many times, they try to make us believe that without them, we would not be able to have these basic needs met. The reason that governments do what they can in this regard is to ensure that they have our support. That support, in many countries, is commonly in the form of votes.

There is NOT a black, white, German, Bangladeshi, Hindu, Jewish, Christian, Conservative, or Liberal way to think. Yes, there are general-purpose statements one can make about specific groups. Catholics do tend to think a certain way about the Pope and birth control. Blacks in America do tend to have certain perceptions about whites and police. Democrats and
Republicans do have general concepts about each other's groups. But, as we mentioned earlier about groups, subgroups, and individual babies, no group of individuals is 100% the same.

A common weakness as individuals is to perceive a group by a few in the group. Some will say something like, "Christianity is such a beautiful thing if it just wasn't for the

Christians. They are so mean." Replace Christianity and Christians with any alternative terms, Islam and Muslims, Judaism and Jews, Buddhism and Buddhists. And it really isn't restricted to religion. Replace those terms with Democratic Party and Democrats, Republican Party and Republicans.

These "normals" include more than just culture. Weather, the color of houses, the social distance between people (not just for medical reasons), and many other differences make up these normals.

We regularly read or hear about extreme behaviors, murders, sexual, physical, or emotional abuse. We feel disturbed that people behave that way. We fail to understand that the range of human emotions and resultant behavior can be that extreme. We seem to think that no one can still behave that way.

Yes, people can be that ignorant, that cruel, that clumsy, that uncaring!

Why is this mentioned? Like many other structures in life, we are susceptible to our consumption of information. The Sunday sermon, our favorite sitcom, or the opinions we hear from coworkers at lunch, our reception of news and how it's presented modifies, diminishes, or reinforces our thoughts and personalities. And, as a result, modifies our behaviors.

The bottom line is recognizing the reasons behind our behaviors.

Compatibility

Compatibility is a challenging subject. Usually, when we think about compatibility, we assume that we're dealing with romantic involvements. Actually, compatibility is a concern in any involvement between two people.

Merriam-Webster states that "compatibility is the ability to exist together in harmony."

The search for compatibility or harmony arises in many relationships. Some of the most common ones occur between family members, coworkers, customers, neighbors, other relatives, church and club members, or classmates. So, with that in mind, we realize that it deals with getting along with anyone, anywhere, anytime.

One's perspective of a relationship sometimes requires a different viewpoint. For example, in many jobs, we deal with what we'll refer to as customers. Customers approach us with needs, typically a product that will give them the ability to deal with a problem. Our job is to provide them with the "thing" that will solve their problem.

Stepping back a bit might open us up to a perception that our "customers" actually include our coworkers or our supervisors. These folks have a problem or need. They are looking to you to provide what they need to solve their problem. In that situation, they may need information or training or a certain task done that you are able to do. So they are looking for something other than what a typical customer might want.

For that matter, we have many other customers. Family members, friends, neighbors, or anyone we meet could be considered customers.

So, how difficult is this? Well, it is harder or easier than we might think.

Our approach begins with exploring the complexity of the personality and resultant behaviors with some tools to gain a better grasp of that complexity.

Because we're discussing relationships, we have to take another look at Maslow's Hierarchy of Needs. See Figure 7-1.

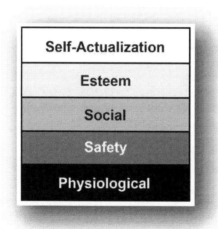

Figure 7-1

We've already talked about the first level, that of physiological or survival needs. As you recall, these are fundamental to our existence, and they apply to everyone. The next level is that of Safety. This is basically the need to provide the basic needs but on an ongoing basis. Typically, this means getting and holding a job that provides the adequate needs to pay for the roof over our heads, food on the table, and clothes on our backs.

Usually, we achieve this by shifting from a "job" to a "career," going from flipping burgers and delivering pizzas to working as a teacher, an administrative assistant, a researcher, an electrician, or some position that gives us a reliable income.

We also need to look at the next step above that, the need to socialize. It is innate in human society that we maintain relationships with other folks. Research has indicated that a certain percentage of working relationships is based on this need to socialize or be with other people. The recent pandemic eliminated some of that socialization, and while it identified situations where some positions did not require people to "come to the office every day," it left a hole in satisfying the interactivity that many people relied on for personal comfort.

An understanding of these needs and our ability to satisfy them are integral to further developing our ability to have some control over compatibility.

While we've discussed how personalities develop, we also need to look at how levels of preferences can impact the complexities of a personality with a view toward compatibility.

While there are several ways of describing the complexity of differences among personalities, we'll use Venn diagrams to clarify them. For those not familiar with Venn diagrams, see Figure 7-2 for an explanation of how they work. The left circle of the diagram represents issue A, while the right circle represents issue B. The area where the circles overlap represents A+B. A+B may represent issues, opinions, behaviors, or any of a variety of components. The overlap represents a combination or a blend of these components.

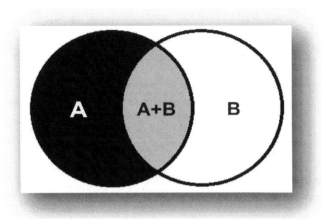

Figure 7-2

For example, let's suppose that issue A is one part of a person's personality while issue B is another part of that same person's personality. The overlap represents compatibility or a compromise between issue A and issue B. In other words, these would be a result of where A and B have merged in the person's personality. The merger of these two issues may also represent a third perspective that might affect other aspects of the personality.

Since a given personality is composed of numerous attitudes, feelings, and beliefs on many issues, the resulting Venn diagram on one person would be more like Figure 7-3.

Each circle represents that person's position on many topics.

Figure 7-3

Wow! Now, we're getting a better idea of a personality's complexity. This is also just scratching the surface of understanding why a person's behavior is so often misunderstood.

Do you remember Sam and Tom from the beginning of the book? Both are likable guys to others, yet they irritate each other in a short amount of time and avoid each other?

Well, each of these circles represents a certain attitude on a topic that is part of Sam's outlook on life. The size of the circle represents how much of Sam's time the issue is thought about. Where its position is in relation to the other issues determines the importance of the issue to Sam. So there's no confusion about these two perspectives; let's assume that Sam's job requires him to spend a lot of time dealing with an issue, but, at the same time, that particular issue is not a critical one in Sam's perspective on life itself.

Refer to Figure 7-4 for the following discussion. We're still talking about Sam. While looking at Sam's personality as Sam 1, imagine that the gray area represents a position level on a given issue. Then, as a result of nudges and shoves, that issue has shifted in intensity within Sam's personality to give us Sam 2.

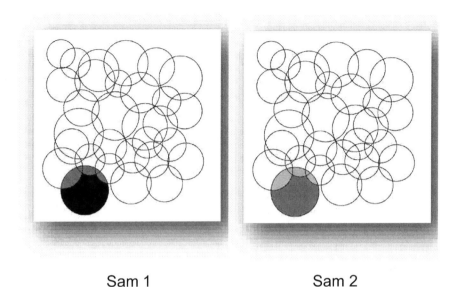

Sam 1   Sam 2

Figure 7-4

The time difference between Sam 1 and Sam 2 may be a few days, a few weeks, or a few years. The point is that Sam has changed his perspective on a given issue.

Let's suppose that it represents a preference for watching a certain sport, such as football. In a relationship, it would indicate that Sam 1 has a certain level of interest in this issue. In Sam 2, it indicates that it is a much higher level of interest.

In a relationship, this preference for football may indicate little difficulty in compatibility. But what if that particular issue was one of religious preference? Then, the difference may represent a major conflict between two people. Even though everything else indicated a complete match on all other topics, because of the differences in this one thing, a comfortable bond between the two personalities may prove to be insurmountable.

Let's take another look at Sam. See Figure 7-5.

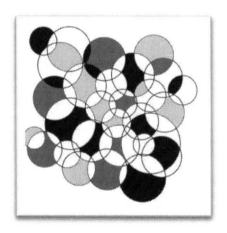

Sam - Figure 7-5

Now, we have an even better perspective on all of the issues that constitute Sam's perspective on life. Keep in mind

that this example represents just a fraction of the issues Sam deals with on a daily, weekly, monthly, yearly basis. Notice that there are also a bunch of different shades of gray. With that in mind, how do we determine compatibility?

Let's take a look at Figure 7-6. On the left, we see Sam and a portion of his outlook on some of the topics he is interested in. On the right is any other person. Hmm. So, what do we do now? It shouldn't be that difficult. After all, you and Sam do this every day, or at least every day that you meet someone else, which is pretty much every day, including Sunday. Maybe even more so on Sunday, depending on which day you set aside for religious observance.

The point is, what do you do? How do we determine the compatibility between Sam and anyone else? More importantly, how do you determine compatibility between YOU and anyone else?

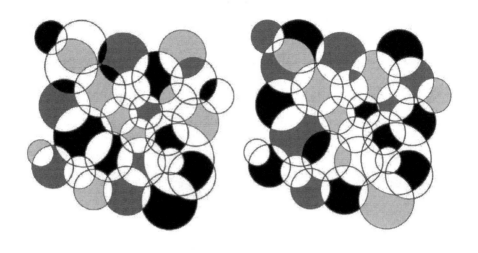

Sam   *Anyone else*

Figure 7-6

How did we first start learning about compatibility? Our initiation into this fascinating and sometimes frustrating area of concern began in our early years. We're going to take a trip down memory lane to get a perspective on the beginning of how we learned about this.

Relationships and associated compatibility began with our parents, typically Mommy and Daddy. As a young child, we began to realize who Mommy and Daddy were. Ideally, there was an impression that Mommy and Daddy were there pretty often. And they always appeared very happy when we saw either one of them.

Of course, as mentioned earlier, sometimes there was someone else, like Nana, Papa, or someone else being our primary caregiver. They also appeared happy when I saw them. Or, maybe they weren't that happy. Maybe they were irritated or in a hurry and didn't spend much time with me.

It's also possible that there were other people around that we later learned lived there, also. They were not big people, bigger than me but not as big as the others. I eventually found out that they were called my brothers and/or my sisters, and we all were part of this thing called a family.

As time went by, we met other people that we were told to call Aunt S or Uncle S. Everyone had a label or name that we used to identify them.

As all of this was going on, we developed some comfort level with all these people. This comfort level was dependent upon the behaviors of these people. How they treated us and how we saw them act around other people had an impact on our feelings of acceptance. This was how our original attitude toward compatibility began.

But there was one more major step in compatibility to be experienced, whether we experienced it during preschool or kindergarten. That exposure to all these other people was our first big challenge in dealing with others.

Preschool or kindergarten was a bit of a shock to many of us. All of a sudden, there were all these other people. There was usually one or two big people who always told us what to do. But then there were also all these other people like you and me, young and busy doing stuff. Depending on how comfortable we were, we got involved in doing things that were fun.

Exercise 7-1

Take a few minutes and think about those early years. Look for one or two of those moments where you remember something distinctive. Maybe it was a birthday party for you or one that you attended. Maybe it was that first day at preschool or kindergarten. Maybe it wasn't the first day but one of the early days. What event stuck out in your mind that dealt with being around those people, either adults or other young ones? What was it about the event that you remember? Why do you think that specific memory stayed in your memory?

And so we began to learn acceptable behaviors around other people. We started our journey into the lifelong practice of compatibility up to where we are now.

Let's take a short break for two more exercises.

Exercise 7-2

Take a moment and determine one behavior that someone else does that irritates you. This may be a term that they use in conversations, a joke that they find funny but insults other people or other groups of people, or a physical behavior such as chewing gum or cracking knuckles. These are just suggestions to help you identify the specific behavior. After you identify one, describe what it is about this that irritates you. Then, determine which folks do not find it irritating. Finally, determine why you are irritated by this behavior and why other folks are not.

Another thing to keep in mind is that because of nudges and shoves if you do these exercises again in five years, you may very well have different answers. And, if you do them again in ten years, you may well have different answers again.

Remember, our personalities are ever-changing.

Exercise 7-3

Take a moment and determine a behavior that you do that you think might irritate others. Use the criteria mentioned in Exercise 7-1 as suggestions. Caution: You may need to ask one or two close friends for assistance in identifying this behavior. After you identify one, describe what it is about it that irritates others. Then, determine which folks do not find it irritating. Finally, determine why some folks are irritated by this behavior and why other folks are not. Again, you may need to consult those friends.

The point of these exercises is to get some idea of how a seemingly trivial behavior can have an impact on relationships. It also provides an insight into the complexity of a person's emotional state and the resultant personality and perceived behaviors. By the way, this includes you.

Also, keeping in mind the ongoing nudges and shoves, the state of flux these issues go through keeps the details of a personality a vibrant and active existence.

Another term we have come to appreciate is professional. Again, we go to Merriam-Webster and find one of the primary definitions of professional to be "exhibiting a courteous, conscientious, and generally businesslike manner in the workplace." In the workplace, acting professionally should be the guiding process. While it's considered to be the responsibility of supervisors and managers to ensure that is the predominant approach, it should be the natural approach coworkers should take with each other. As long as the focus is on getting processes or tasks accomplished politely and respectfully, there should be little or no difficulty in collaborating with each other.

In other relationships, such as school, church, shopping, etc., the golden rule of "do unto others as you would have done unto you" should be more than adequate.

With all of this in mind, the challenge of compatibility may, at a glance, seem insurmountable.

Fortunately, because of a human's awesome flexibility, it is not.

At this point, we also want to discuss a concept called Johari Windows, Figure 7-7. This concept was developed by psychologists Joseph Luft (1916–2014) and Harrington Ingham (1916–1995) in 1955. The name was a shortened version of their last names. It was designed to provide a perception of ourselves.

The Johari windows cover four areas involving the perceptions of you. The first window, labeled "Open to All," consists of what you know about yourself that others also know.

The second window, "Hidden," is what you know about yourself that others do not know; the third, "Blind Spot," is what others know about you that you don't know, and finally, "Unknown," is what neither you nor others know about you.

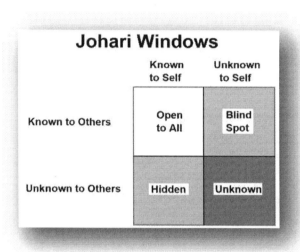

Figure 7-7

The first three windows may seem self-explanatory. But, you should put some thought into them to get a better understanding of them. The fourth window is interesting in that it is difficult to imagine what would be there. One concept is that it might contain a hidden talent or aptitude. You may not have experienced an event that would trigger an awareness or an interest that you had never thought about before.

Thinking about or using the Johari Windows gives us another tool to use when examining our relationships with others.

Exercise 7-4

Using the Johari Window format, try to determine some traits or behaviors that you would file under each window. When you come to the window about things others notice about you that you don't know, you should find a close friend with whom your relationship is good and whose opinion you value. You may find something that pleases you. But, of course, you may also find out something that concerns you.

Obviously, the Unknown window will be somewhat challenging.

Now, let's take a look at what we normally think of about compatibility, the romantic version.

Before we go any further, this is another occasion where we need to understand what we're not going to do. There are no profile-matching processes or magically winning combinations. Those who are looking for that approach can find innumerable books on the topic or apps for that purpose.

Some cultures have stringent criteria that must be applied to meeting and mating with someone. Some places use astrology to match a couple for the forever after. There's numerology and biorhythms for those who are so inclined.

There's always that old saying of "opposites attract." Now, there might be some validity to the statement and it may have its intrinsic charm or fascination in the beginning, but after a while, that charm can turn into irritation or frustration as one begins to wonder why the other "just can't see the light" while the other wonders why "he/she is so uptight" about an issue.

Another way to look at the issue of compatibility is to think of it as preparing a dish for a meal for someone. The dish has a recipe, including the necessary ingredients and the directions for preparing it.

Unfortunately, we may not have all of the ingredients in our pantry.

One of the groups where the relationships have more impact, is within the family. Relations between brothers, sisters, husband and wife, fathers or mothers with sons or daughters can carry more weight.

Now What!?

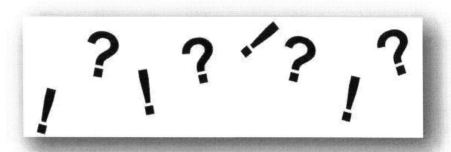

Here we are! Now what?

We know that our personality starts before birth. We know that the expectant mother's life during pregnancy has an impact on the early formation of our personality.

We know that even twins will have ever so slightly different bases of personality upon birth. And, of course, even in the case of twins, there are still the tedious, repetitious statements of "I'm first…," "He/she is the oldest…," statements that will set the relationship of senior/junior. The phrases that will require internal study and thought to establish one's real status as a person.

We know that upon our birth, we have already set a base on our personality that future events will build on and mold, intensely at first, but continually, gently, or strongly, for every day of our life.

We have also realized that, at any point in time, we have the ability to evaluate our circumstances, weigh the possible outcomes of our decision at the moment, and make that decision with an understanding of our justification for that decision.

Whew! Now that we know all that, life is going to be so much easier. Right? Yeah, right.

Because everyone has lived a different life, born with a different base, impacted with countless series of nudges and shoves different from yours, every decision you make and act on will be disagreed with by a bunch of folks. These disagreeing opinions may include several from folks close to you. These people may well be parents, siblings, aunts, uncles, grandparents, and best friends.

Now, keep in mind that some of those close to you may well be in complete agreement with your decision and resultant action. They will support you all the way. Or, maybe they will support you some of the way.

The whole point is that there will always be those who agree with your decision, and there will always be those who disagree. They do not have to live with your decision, but you do. You will always be responsible for your decision.

We've discussed the cause and effect of our decision several times, but it must be repeated here.

"If it wasn't for (enter name here) saying/doing/repeating/insulting/praising/complimenting (enter second name here), then I wouldn't have had to say/do that."

At this point, we realize that it's all up to you. We didn't make (enter names and actions here). It's not their behaviors that control you. It's your reactions, which are based on your decisions, that control you.

If you've done the exercises, you have a better sense of where you are now, compared to where you were in Chapter 1. If you skipped the exercises, you may have a bit of a better idea, but not as much. As we said way back in the commercial break, you need to put some time and effort into answering the questions you were asked in those exercises.

So, where do you go from here? You've seen how personality starts before you are born. After the swat on the bottom that made you realize that your life had just been turned upside down, you struggled to make sense of this new environment.

In the beginning, everything that happened was happening in an alien universe.

You've realized that the events in the early years had a major impact on setting the tone of your perceptions.

Age brings perspective. The more you learn, the more you realize there is so much more to learn. There have been movies where the lead actor has gone back in time. The interesting aspect is that when they go back in time, they do so with all of the accumulated knowledge they have collected since that time they went back. The obvious thing the movie makes a point of is that we realize we would have acted differently had we had that knowledge. As a result, we should realize that we will continue to learn new things as each day, week, month, and year goes by.

We realize that the longer a person has been on a job, the more proficient he/she becomes. They are not only better at the assigned tasks but have also developed an awareness of details and are more capable of determining what is or is not relevant. This is perspective, and it only comes with time.

It's the same with life. The longer we've been around, the better is our perspective. But it's important to remember that the ability to improve that perspective only occurs when we pay attention to our surroundings and behaviors.

On top of that, we now realize that many behaviors can easily become routine, and we can fall into the trap of going on automatic pilot. We can fall into that trap of complacency. That complacency, while very effective for efficiency, tends to blunt our attention. The echo chamber concept, while seemingly efficient, can also be a seductive trap that many fall into.

Actually, most of us have succumbed to that head-in-the-clouds attitude at one point in time or another. Sometimes, it takes one of those shoves referred to earlier to jar us back into awareness.

You have an understanding of needs and the totem pole on which they're based. You realize you don't need that new, high-def TV, nice as it is. You have the basics: food, clothing, and a roof over your head.

Having satisfied your needs, one of the goals is to determine how to prioritize and satisfy your wants.

You realize now that you really only know many people by their reputation. You now know that all saints were sinners, and even the sinners have their moments of sainthood.

So, now what?!

"Now" is now and "what" is up to you.

We've attempted to arm you with some tools for thought. The thinking is your strength, and the tools provided here will enable you to use your strength more effectively.

You learned early that no one knows you well enough to judge you or your behavior. As a result, I hope you've come to understand that you are not wise enough to even consider judging another. That's why there was the earlier suggestion that you should practice unjudging.

Evaluate your own attitude, thoughts, and behavior. Everyone has a bad day, but that is not an excuse for bad behavior. The event does NOT control your behavior; YOU DO! – NOW WHAT!? = Your decision. If you have a question at this point, go back to Chapter 1 and see what you missed or misunderstood.

Now, what do you do next? What is this all about in the first place or, better yet, in the next place?

First of all, we have discovered that, out of the several billion people in the world, just about any type of personality and associated behavior actually exists. We simply do not recognize what some of these behaviors caused by these personalities might be until we actually see them or personally experience a relationship with them. While we can and do read about them or hear friends and relatives recount various events with notable behaviors and reactions, we usually do not attach much importance to them. It's only when we are personally involved that we feel the value of the event and how we decide to react to it.

As discussed, emotion is an integral part of our learning about the various aspects of life. Emotion has a varying impact on different events we experience. As previously stated, we rarely experience an emotional effect when reading about someone's behavior or listening to a friend or relative's experience. It's only when we observe it firsthand that it delivers a learning point.

Remember, you can never go back. Time travel is not a viable option at this point in time. Even if it were, it would still not be the same. But, for discussion purposes, if you went back in time now, you would not be the same person you were at that point in time. You are not the same person you were ten years ago. And you will not be the same person ten years from now.

While the movies have done admirably humorous depictions of the possibilities, it can be reasonably assumed that it isn't going to happen.

So, now what? What has been discovered in the few chapters here that we can strap on to our decision part of the brain? Well, let's see.

Here are some suggested behaviors you might consider practicing.

Listen to understand, not to reply. When having a conversation with someone, one of the many traps we fall into is waiting to say something as soon as the other person pauses. Instead of immediately talking, ensure you understand what the other one is saying. You might even start your reply by repeating what you understood them to say. This serves two purposes.

First, it ensures that you hear them correctly. Second, it shows that you respect them by confirming to them that you are paying attention.

Since most of what we have learned is based on something we read or heard from someone else, we should start our statement with "I read…," "I heard…," or "I thought…." This is intended to declare that the statement is open for discussion. By stating something as if it was a fact makes it sound like a challenge, or a fact when we may not really know for sure.

Play devil's advocate (politely disagree). Even if you agree, it helps to make your brain work. One of the activities in high school is debate class. The primary function of debate class is to be able to defend either side of a response to a question. This requires studying the question and gaining enough information about what the possible responses might be. By playing devil's advocate, you are automatically forcing the other person to defend their statement, their viewpoint.

Obviously, you will want to do this in a tactful, respectful manner. You might initiate the talk with the phrase, "Just for discussion, I would suggest that…," and then make your statement which offers an alternative to theirs. It's important to remember that there are no intended winners or losers in the process. The purpose is to expand your learning to accept that there are alternatives to suggested actions.

The final suggestion is, REMEMBER! Remember,

everyone thinks a certain way because it is their normal, based on their life. It is going to be different from your normal.

Regardless of the level of complexity in your relationships with other folks, there are things you will not know about them. During their life, there were always things that occurred behind closed doors.

These suggestions are intended to help you maintain perspective on your perceptions of things and the perceptions of your friends, relatives, and other associates.

And remember, you're not going to have a good relationship with everybody. Remember Tom and Sam, two great guys whose company everyone enjoyed. But, they didn't care to be around each other for more than a few minutes? Personalities are those webs of preferences, likes, and dislikes that everyone has. That complexity is going to create irritation among some people. Accept it, maintain respect for those differences, and move on in life.

We've all had moments of great pleasure and happiness about the results of our decisions. But, remember that we've also had moments of concern about our decisions. We've suffered moments of anguish about them.

The important thought to take away is that everyone else has experienced those same thoughts and feelings. So, if their behavior seems to be out of line or just plain odd, we must realize that they may well be experiencing similar concerns or frustrations in those moments. Therefore, a little patience would be appreciated. As the old saying goes, we're all in this together.

In every individual's life, there exists an immense amount of knowledge, of experience, of relationships, of perceptions.

So, when a person passes away, a small universe disappears.

Exercise 8.1

Review the exercises in the previous chapters. You may consider some of them to become habits, as the answers will change as the years go by. Remember, no one has all the answers. All of life is a learning experience.

And remember, think about your thinking…

About the Author

Bob Bruno had a very diverse career path encompassing fields as varied as portrait photography, inventory control management, programming, web-based training, and technical writing among others. He retired as a Chief in the U.S. Navy

He was the stage director for three beauty pageants with the winners going directly to the Miss World and Miss Universe pageants. Bob also entertained as a juggler with swords and fireballs in night clubs and small carnivals.

All of this required a keen observation of human behavior, supported by studies in Sociology and Human Resource Development.

The most immediate result is his writing "Saints & Sinners, Geniuses & Idiots: Now What!?".

The book is an explanatory, self-help endeavor that explores your personality, how it started, how it developed, and your ability to control its expression.

bobbruno.net

bob@bobbruno.net

Made in the USA
Columbia, SC
01 July 2025

b888fccb-5ffa-479f-9ada-8f0ce04609ffR02